A Life
(Most Definitely)
Less Ordinary

Stuart Hepburn

What they said about "A Most Curious Detour."

'Emotional, heartbreaking, funny, inspirational. A must-read for everyone. Highly recommended.'

'I read this over and over during my cancer scare.'

'A gift to the world.'

'A shining light in the darkest corner.'

'This book touched all of my emotions.'

'Two things emerge having read this book; that the human spirit is incredibly powerful and that our stories are a key tool for transformation. I recommend that you read it.'

'Stuart's book connected with me in quite unexpected ways. A real find. I'm enriched by taking the detour with him.'

CONTENTS

ACKNOWLEDGMENTS

Writing a book was a marathon task for me, so I couldn't have done it without very dedicated support. First, there's Pam, my wife, who has been my loyal supporter for the last 26 years, and who read through several drafts of this material, beyond the point where it made any sense. Then there's my personal assistant, Monika Knitter who has added a new dimension to what's possible in my life. There's James Lennox (Slo-Hand Jimmy Cool) who helped with the photography, eventually. Alasdair Kane who tore himself away from Godfrey, his pet tortoise for just long enough to help with the publishing. And Sharon and the gang at Longstone Day Centre provided a great deal of support and encouragement, and more than a few cups of tea. The Centre is managed by one of the best managers I have come across, Linda Gibson (shame about her OT roots though!) 😜

Last but by no means least, the support team at Blackwood who make it possible for me to function on a daily basis. And my life will not be worth living if I don't mention the Greek Mermaid, Nicole.

INTRODUCTION

This project started out as a book on the benefits of yoga. But what I think will be read more widely is a warts-and-all story of the life of someone who tried to follow a rather unusual path. As a result, I have set out some of the emotional turmoil that I experienced on my particular path. I have done so in the hope that you can learn from my mistakes, which have been plentiful. (Just ask my wife).

I know that when I started to read books covering some of the issues in this book, a major concern was to assess the credibility of the authors. In writing this material I realise that I am putting myself up for that same assessment. By putting the details of my whole life out there I also realise that there's a lot of potential for critical comments, so pardon me if I feel a little vulnerable.

I realise also that in putting my beliefs and experiences on paper there is lots of scope for causing offence to those who hold different beliefs or who follow different practices. This is certainly not what I intend to achieve so I hope that you are able to read this book and fully enjoy it.

This book will take you across continents and through some unusual territory. So, dust off your passports and get ready for the ride.

CHAPTER 1.   MIDLIFE CRISIS

The term "life changing injury" is heard quite regularly in the media. But I wonder if you've ever stopped to think deeply about what it means? There's a sense in which all experience is life changing by virtue of the events we experience on a daily basis, because our lives are continuously honed by our experiences. So, what's the big deal about a life changing injury?

Well, for some people at least, a life changing injury is like waking up to find that you are not the same person you were when you went to sleep. Your identity has completely changed. Your stock of knowledge may have changed, your skill set, even the basic things like swallowing and potty training may have disappeared. Your place in the family may have gone. Your ability to communicate, or to communicate effectively, may have ended. And maybe worst of all, your ability to contribute to the communal tapestry of life in a meaningful way may have gone. (And before someone else says it let me concede that it may not have.)

It was a brain-stem stroke in 2005 that did it for me. If, like me at the time, you don't know what a stroke is, it's to do with blocked or leaky blood flow in the brain, usually leading to death or some form of disability. I still remember the haunted faces of my fellow brain-injured patients as they wandered the hospital corridors wondering who they had become, terrified at the prospect of trying to re-engage with an immensely complex world that didn't cater much for 'passengers.'

Immediately after my stroke there were a few days spent in a coma, probably an induced coma, followed by what seemed like an eternity spent in a frozen, locked-in body, with no speech whatsoever. Even a little itch on my foot could trigger a major panic as I would suddenly realise that I was powerless to respond. Nor could I direct the attention of the doctors to any specific problems I might be experiencing. Cramp was a major dread. It had always been solved by some kind of social interaction, but under the circumstances, that was out of the question. And I couldn't even change position to ease the pain which compounded my sense of powerlessness and spiked my anxiety.

At this point, I feel it's important to be clear about what I am setting out to achieve. Your sympathy and empathy are not going to help anyone. And for me to simply depress you with my tales of woe is not going to leave you in a very resourceful state. So that's a lose-lose situation for everyone!

It's very important to me that you take something of value from reading this book, and that it does more than give you another reason to feel sad. My purpose in writing this book is to direct you towards the question 'what happens when the body breaks down? What is the part that is left?' Now, there will be different ideas about this, and that's not a problem. I'm going to offer you my take on the situation, and perhaps it will give you food for thought. There again, perhaps not!

A recent survey of Scottish opinion* suggests that Scots are turning their backs on the conventional belief systems promoted by the main religions. Let me say at the outset that I totally concur with this trend. For far too long we have unthinkingly followed the guidance of 'professionals,' delegating our responsibility to think about these difficult issues for ourselves and failing to manage our own 'spirituality.' As a consequence, even religions have become more materialistic and the potential for spirituality in each of us has become largely dormant.

But when you are lying in a bed with a completely paralysed body these matters come sharply to your attention in a way that perhaps they wouldn't in a busy household. I have meditated since 1976 and curiously, it was only after my stroke, when I probably needed it most, that I lost the ability to meditate. I don't know if you have ever noticed but hospitals are very noisy places, with continuous beeping of hungry drips, the constant clatter of miscellaneous large metal objects, and the never-ending dramas of ward life. On my last visit to hospital in 2018, a complete stranger came into my room on a daily basis and sat down to chat as though I was his best friend. He would enter with a big smile and greet me with a name I didn't recognise, before asking for my progress report. I presume he was a victim of dementia but it tested my ability to stay in rapport.

Eighteen months in hospital was a long time to go without meditation and during my stay I had succumbed to the general misery that is hospital life. If truth were told, I had become a curmudgeon, a grumpy old man. I had become reliant on meditation as a way of refreshing my focus on what was important to me, and how I wanted to be in my life. It was true my outlook on life had, very gradually, become somewhat 'Christianised' over the years, through the influence of the broadly accepted notions of 'right' and 'wrong.'

But nevertheless, meditation had become an indispensable part of my routine and the loss of it, in the midst of my hospital trauma, was a big loss to me. I remember awakening one morning to the sound of a TV. Someone was interviewing holidaymakers at a caravan park encouraging them to participate in some mindless and humiliating games. I remember feeling as though I was wading through treacle. This was not an environment I wanted to be in.

Talking of treacle, another sticky issue here will be mention of God in this book. (Thought that might shock you!) I know it's not very fashionable to refer to God. Most of my friends and acquaintances would claim to have outgrown the concept of a God in much the same way as they have outgrown their beliefs in Santa Claus. It's true that science has liberated many, young people in particular, from the chains of the world's major religions and in stepping away from religions the concept of a God has also been abandoned except in emergencies like critical injuries.

However, even in societies that have actively tried to usurp notions of a God, like the Soviet Union and communist China, it has been found necessary to reverse their policy as a means of permitting people to deepen their experience of purpose and meaning beyond the material level of technology and science.

Let's get back to me in my hospital bed. You can see my dilemma. I was struggling in a body that wouldn't work, with aspirations to go beyond the consciousness of the body. A nurse on the ward confirmed to me that the part of the brain that had been damaged was the part I would need for meditation. If that was true, then it wasn't just the hostile environment of the hospital ward that prevented me from meditating but my tuning button had also been damaged, and I had been left like a radio without a functioning tuner.

It occurred to me that I had maybe just lost the belief in my ability to move my body, and that if I changed my beliefs then perhaps my body would move after all. I tried asking myself the question: what if I could move my limbs if I really tried? I remember straining every sinew in the attempt to move a leg, but nothing even stirred. I couldn't move the body and I couldn't escape the consciousness of the body. I felt well and truly snookered!

It's perhaps not surprising that against this background my mind began to explore some deep issues that we normally manage to avoid by being busy with everyday matters. Urgent but not necessarily important, as we used to say on time management courses.

I began thinking about my relationship with my now paralysed body. Initially the doctors had decided that there was little evidence of brain activity judging from my scans, to the ex-tent that they wanted to withdraw clinical support if my condition continued to deteriorate. I felt I was the same character I had always been with the same beliefs and values. I had the same sense of humour. In fact, one of the most difficult aspects of having no voice was that I couldn't contribute one-liners that would have changed things in difficult scenarios. So how was it possible that the doctors had got it so wrong? Had the equipment been faulty or had they just missed something? Or was it a conspiracy to get rid of me, my paranoid, morphine-ingested self wondered.

After the acute phase of my illness I was transferred to a rehabilitation hospital. My body also began to recover, to a very limited extent. My right arm, although weak, could move within a very limited range and some laboured speech began to emerge from my mouth. After the acute phase of my illness someone asked for my help to do some work at National level in Malawi. Without thinking it through, I immediately began to announce that I was going to work in Malawi once I was discharged. Needless to say, I would have struggled to get to Edinburgh Airport let alone Malawi at the time, I had no clear understanding of how my life was about to change and probably had some residual hope that by some miracle I would recover sufficiently to simply pick up where I had left off two years previously, before my stroke.

I had long been familiar with the concept of a non-physical entity, or soul, since going to view the recently deceased body of my father who had died suddenly of heart disease at the age of 47. I suppose I had wanted to be with him one last time. On entering the room where his body lay, I found my aunt deep in conversation with the body on display. With a quick glance, I could see that the one I had known as my father was no longer there and that the body laid out before me held no interest for me whatsoever. Perhaps this was my first introduction to the concept of a soul. I have no doubt that there are many other interpretations of this situation, but that's mine!

When I was discharged from my rehab hospital after eighteen months there was a tremendous sense of relief. I hadn't recognised it fully at the time, but as I chilled in the garden of my new supported home, with the breeze, at long last, blowing through my hair, I realised just how traumatic the hospital stay had been for me. Trauma is such a routine part of hospital life that it becomes normalised after a while. And now it was all behind me, or so I thought. In fact, the most traumatic part was still to come!

After just three days I was rushed back to a third hospital, with a case of gangrene. And if that wasn't bad enough my hospital consultant announced that they had found symptoms of pneumonia and MRSA too. I wasn't too happy about dealing with the three conditions simultaneously. In fact, my mind was turning back to thoughts about the eternal soul. It looked like I might be parting company with the mortal coil much sooner than I'd expected!

Two collapsed lungs, acute renal failure, and several minutes of clinical death later, I found myself ensconced in yet another hospital bed. This time I was slightly more grateful to be there, and I had good reason to be. It was to be another three months before I was discharged from that final hospital, and heading back to my deserted new flat. This time I was more nervous. I knew that death could strike at any time. Intellectually we all know that but knowing it as a death 'veteran' seemed to make it a more real prospect. At night time I would go to bed with the very real prospect of awakening to find myself no longer in the body with which I had become so familiar.

My timeline before my stroke had stretched out straight in front of me, disappearing over a hill only at the onset of old age. I wonder if that's what they mean by being 'over the hill'? But now my timeline stretched no further than the following week. It was im-possible for me to plan ahead, for holidays for example, as I couldn't see myself that far in the future. Fortunately, this scenario passed with time and, like most normal people, I now go to sleep with the assumption that I will still be in the same body in the morning. My timeline has also reappeared, although much shorter than it once was, and more speculative.

My anxiety, on my return to the big world was not confined to matters relating to death. An even bigger concern related to life. What could I meaningfully achieve through a body that offered me just one working arm, and a weak one at that? This was full-blown existential anxiety. In the absence of my meditation I felt off-balance and purposeless. The walls of my flat seemed to close in on me.

For someone who had previously travelled fairly extensively my world had become very small.

The undoubted hero of these dark days was my wife. During this time, I was totally reliant on her unwavering support, a support that has continued through to the present day I'm very glad to say. It raises for me real questions about how much support is provided for the partners of patients in the midst of traumatic life-changing events. While I was surrounded in hospital by the best care available my wife was grieving the loss of her partner's former identity and taking on the task of sole manager of all household matters. This was a big ask!

Immediately after the stroke we communicated through blinks, but as I began to very slowly recover, I was given a typing device similar to the one used by Stephen Hawking and with the same electronic voice which I jokingly used to use as evidence of my close family relationship to Stephen Hawking. By using my voice box, I was able to send brief messages to my wife, but it certainly never extended into a deep conversation. My wife would probably add at this point that it never had!

About this time, and against this background, I rediscovered my ability to meditate. Who knows how? Immediately, hidden knots deep in my body began to unwind. I was back on track. Let me tell this story from the beginning.

* Reference

Survey of Scottish Beliefs. 2018. The Humanist Society

CHAPTER 2.   THE SEEDS OF CHANGE

My family background was what you might call traditional working class, with uncles who were glaziers, shoe repairers, and cousins who were van drivers, electricians and the like. My father escaped all this by training as an engineer and then serving in World War II as a junior officer in the navy. His social ascendancy was further reinforced when he later started his own very successful business, installing central heating at a time when virtually everyone was turning away from burning coal in their homes. He also offered more conventional plumbing and electrical services. At its peak, his firm employed about forty people.

It was his dream that we children should be well schooled in order that we could contribute to the business at a later date. I regarded him with some awe. My own personal war hero with even a scar on his neck where he had been wounded by a bullet during the war. He was a strongly principled employer and also quite charismatic, winning the respect of most of those who knew him. So, I was very willing to go along with his long-term aspirations because working with him was quite an attractive prospect for me.

As a consequence, at the age of five I found myself at one of Edinburgh's foremost fee-paying schools. What I encountered there was a privileged world that was quite alien to me. I was invited to birthday parties in big mansions where both parents were professors. I remember that when it came to my turn to throw a party one person said, in a matter of fact way, "This is the first time that I've been in an ordinary house".

The author at school, (standing in the centre, right of teacher).

As I moved through the school, I ended up with a form master who used to refer to me as 'the plumber' and who beat me regularly for 'forgetting a tool'. Of course, he wouldn't get away with that these days but at the time it was par for the course. I remember once having an eye infection and receiving a very public lecture from him about the dangers of not washing. If his aim was to make me feel small it certainly worked. He was an ex-pupil of the same school and he clearly resented the arrival in the school of 'les nouveau riche.' The rigidity of the class system was inexorably beginning to crumble. When I eventually left school, I was described in the school magazine as one of the most 'industrial' pupils in the sixth year.

With school behind me, I had time to reflect on the world of privilege I had experienced and knew that it was a world in desperate need of change. Even though I was still intent on taking my place in the business world I knew that it would have to be business in a new way. And I had some ideas about how that could be achieved in a commercially successful way.

My time at the University of Edinburgh did nothing to change my mind. Business Studies and Accountancy seemed the most direct route to become useful for the family business. But during my study of economics I came across my first point of conflict with the world of business. According to classical economic theory, businesses should relocate wherever 'the factors of production' labour, materials, transport to market, are minimised. Thus, for example, James Dyson recently decided to relocate his business to the Philippines because labour costs are significantly lower there.

In the political environment of the early '70s, which was much more militant than it is now, I became agitated by the fact that 'social costs,' the costs to the local community, were not considered a relevant factor to be included in the conventional business equation. I met with the economics lecturer and put it to him that there was a key consideration missing from the classical economics model and therefore that he ought to modify the model he was going to present to our class. We weren't afraid to challenge the status quo in those days, though by today's standards it may appear somewhat outrageous.

When the time came, he didn't make any significant changes and so I stood up and, for the first time ever, walked out of a lecture. To my surprise, about half the class of about thirty followed me out of the room. This was the first time that my politics had been acted out and perhaps the first time I knew that I wanted my life to be about changing things towards, what I regarded, as a fairer and more compassionate world. It was a very small incident but it played a key part in my understanding of the sort of impact I wanted to make in the world.

If I was to enter the family business, it would have to

become a high wage, 'intelligent' workplace, where results would be achieved by respect and self-motivation. I was just beginning to see the direction that I wanted to move towards. But all of that was about to be blown apart by a development that I had not seen coming. It was on the eve of my first-year exams. I was well prepared although understandably nervous.

My father had come home as usual for his lunch when he complained of a sharp pain in his chest. He had a history of heart problems so I wasn't overly concerned. An ambulance eventually arrived after what seemed like an age and he disappeared into hospital in much the same way as he had several times before, with my mother accompanying him. I knew the routine, after all, I had been making hospital visits since I was a small child. I wasn't fazed by developments. I even got back to my last-minute revision for the first-year exams which would surely tell me if I was on track with my studies, something you can never be sure of in the first year at university.

But all that changed in an instant when a small party of hospital 'escorts' returned to the door with the news that my father had died. It had never entered my head that such a thing was possible. I had simply assumed that once in the hands of the doctors he would be safe. My whole world collapsed around my ears. The one person around whom I had built my world was gone and my world didn't make sense any more. I was devastated by the situation.

I now experienced a bit of a crisis, in my life generally and also specifically in my course selection. I suddenly found myself on a university course that no longer held the slightest interest for me. But what else could I do? At school I had excelled in two subjects, Art and English. Neither of these two subjects were regarded with any great respect in my home. Perhaps if I had been bolder, I would have made the giant leap into one of these two courses.

In reality, I stood in the queue for my Business Studies lecture and noticed how uninspiring it was. Alongside me there were two other queues. One was for Social Anthropology and the other for Sociology. The Social Anthropology queue was comprised of a group of individuals dressed predominantly in ethnic clothing. My very quick and unscientific judgement was that these were not people who would change the world. By contrast the Sociology queue looked both fun and possessing a gravitas that suggested that things in the real world could be changed. At that moment my mind was made up. I was switching to Sociology. My tutor was appalled and warned of significantly lower earnings. He was right there, and with hindsight, a career in anthropology might have been quite satisfying.

And so, in 1971 I embarked on a four-year Sociology degree with the vague intention of moving into a social work career. When I joined a social work class though, I changed my mind. The class was full of, in my eyes at the time, unthinking left-wing prejudice. These people wanted to rearrange the deck chairs not build a new ship. At that time, for me, they were part of the problem, not part of its solution. Today they might be labelled 'Blairites'.

In my new course I inevitably came across the writings of Karl Marx and for the first time I had a comprehensive theory of how change might take place. Today Marx's writings on the development of socialism have been largely debunked. Although his analysis of the limitations of capitalism are still alive and kicking. As a consequence, it is hard to grasp how influential Marx was in the '70s. The term "Marxist" at last provided me with a label that allowed me to understand my role in a much bigger picture.

But there was one further influence I took from my university days and probably one that was later to play a significant part later in my life. In 1974 I was introduced by a philosophy student to the notion of existentialism. I can only give you my take on this philosophy as it's a bit hard to provide a single definition that is comprehensive. Existentialism for me was about awakening to the fact that I was spinning a single thread all the way through my life, one that I was totally responsible for and one that could not be simply abandoned in the face of a broader ideology. The practical result of all this was that even though I happily adopted the term 'Marxist' I continued to paddle my own canoe, that's to say, I continued to think for myself.

That said, by the time I had finished my degree in 1975 I was quite firm in my radical political outlook. Even an invitation to do post-graduate work at the University of California in Los Angeles held no attraction for me. At the time, that seemed like a self-indulgent distraction from the real struggle that was rapidly unfolding here in Britain.

I was now certain my life would be about changing things for the better with little doubt about the kind of change that was necessary. Leaving behind a mystified girlfriend who had held the promise of a comfortable and safe future, I set off instead for London where a life of action seemed more likely. With hindsight, I now recognise the pain that my abrupt departure must have caused to the poor girl in question. My focus at the time was quite narrow.

At first, I stayed with a university chum who was based in a modern tower block in Mile End. From his apartment on one of the top floors I was able to see the vast scale of the city that was to be my home for the next five years. In the mid '70s the skyline of London was very different from today's London. There were far fewer high-rise buildings in the city centre and much more industry, with chimneys and factories in abundance. Perhaps the prevalence of cranes was a sign of things to come.

Somehow or other, I don't remember exactly how, I was introduced to a group of politically like-minded lads who lived together not far from Ladbroke Grove, a much more central location. When they mentioned that they had a spare bedroom at their place I leapt at the opportunity. It was only when I arrived at the flat, with two bags containing my worldly possessions, that I discovered that it was a squat that I was moving into. It was a three storey terraced building, part of a pre-war row of houses just off Ladbroke Grove. The bedroom that I was allocated was quite small, equipped with a bare mattress which lay on the uncovered floorboards. It wasn't the start that I had envisaged but I felt fortunate to have a base from which to explore and a ready-made circle of politically like-minded friends.

I wouldn't have chosen to live in a squat but neither did it concern me too much. I suppose at the time I managed to see it as a legitimate statement of intent to redistribute resources though I have a very different perspective today. I suppose at the time the inequalities were more starkly apparent than they are today.

We would gather daily in the room designated as 'the kitchen,' a small, bare room with a wooden table, and digest the daily news which surely offered absolute proof that capitalism, across the board, was on its knees. We weren't active in any way, just content to await the inevitable end of a system that had generated so many problems for so many people.

One thing which did concern me was the fact that things were going missing from the fridge. Anybody who has shared a flat will be familiar with this scenario. But it wasn't the missing items that concerned me, so much as the fact that everybody in the flat denied responsibility. I had an opportunity to think about the nature of private property and the morality of simply "liberating" things at will. But what disturbed me most about all this were the looks of innocence on everybody's faces when I raised the topic. Even amongst this small group of 'comrades' there was dishonesty. Things got even worse when a physical fight broke out at the foot of the stairs about to whom a certain girl 'belonged'.

I was rapidly coming to the conclusion that my flat mates were essentially no different from the rest of the population except that they had been excluded from the rewards of the current economic system and were now awaiting the spoils of its dying carcass. I was familiar with the bit of the Marxist theory which predicted that 'natural man' would not fully emerge until a just economic system had been fully established. But I couldn't even see green shoots emerging from this particular group of house-mates.

And so, day after day, we would simply gather and speculate on how long it would be before the entire system would collapse. One interesting exception to this rule was a tall and sturdy lad from Northern Ireland who took no part in these discussions. In fact, he didn't take part in any of our activity. You might think that this would have made him a topic of conversation in the house but in fact he remained curiously anonymous. And this despite the fact that he locked the door to his bedroom when he went out and that Irish politics was being played out on the streets of London at the time. I guess I'll never know but I do wonder at our lack of 'revolutionary' curiosity.

I decided to use my fixed abode as an opportunity to apply for a job as a bus driver with London Transport. It was a major shock when I was turned down at interview for being 'overqualified' It had never occurred to me that I might not be welcomed with open arms as something of a coup for London Transport. Having been poorly treated at school by those enjoying privilege it dawned on me that I couldn't expect a warm welcome from those who had been excluded from that privilege either.

In mild desperation, I filled in a second application for London Transport but this time in east London, and with no mention of my degree. To my amazement they conducted a computer search, at a time when no-one had a computer, and discovered my hidden past. Once again, the door slammed on me!

When I did eventually get a job in a warehouse the problem continued. This time it was because of my reading material. Without giving it a thought, I had brought my usual newspaper into work. Apparently, this caused a stir because it wasn't a red-top and established a rocky relationship with my co-workers, a relationship which never really recovered from this initial breach of trust, and one that helped me to understand that there was a working-class culture that I found to be just as exclusive as the culture I had encountered at school. For the first time, I encountered 'reverse snobbery' where 'knowing things' was frowned upon and fitting into a narrow range of behaviour, like going to the pub or holidaying at a popular location, seemed to be essential for social acceptance.

All this was beginning to disillusion me. I couldn't see a way forward. There were no obvious examples of individuals 'walking the talk'. A quote from Mahatma Gandhi caught my attention. "Be the solution you want to see in the world." I decided to read more of Gandhi's philosophy and this in turn led me to other Eastern writers. I read them with genuine excitement. Here was morality being set out as a vehicle for social change. Quite different to Marx's approach but with a similar end; social justice. Marx had described religion as 'the opium of the people' so I was treading very carefully in this alien territory.

By this time, I was beginning to feel a bit stressed. I was still living in a Marxist squat, with a group of 'friends' who were, outwardly at least, following a very different path to the one I was embarking on. I had also recently been through the trauma of my finals at university. It seemed like a good time to take up a relaxing pastime like

Hatha Yoga. Accordingly, I let it be known that I was interested in finding a yoga teacher and I was given the name of an Egyptian man named Kamal who lived nearby, on Ladbroke Grove. I didn't know anything about him other than that he 'did yoga'. I had no information about the kind of yoga he did or where he taught. I didn't even know if he was looking for students. So, my next step was highly speculative.

CHAPTER 3. KAMAL

I climbed several stairs just a hundred metres from the house where I was living and nervously pressed his bell. I didn't know what to expect and felt seriously outside my comfort zone with the topic of yoga about which I knew nothing. In fact, I was beginning to hope he was out and that I could walk away with a clear conscience. But these thoughts were suddenly interrupted when an overhead light clicked on and the door burst open to reveal the figure of a short, stocky man with glasses. He was probably around thirty, with a light skin and a slightly flattened face that I believe is quite common in Egyptians.

"Come in" he said, "I've been expecting you." There was something about the way he said that which unnerved me even more. It was as if he already knew I was coming. I stepped through a short hallway and into his ground-floor room. He had a small kitchen off to the left where he brewed up teas for us both. His flat was comprised of those two rooms plus a narrow corridor leading to his bedroom.

He then returned and sat opposite me. After the usual exchange of pleasantries, we got down to the reason for my visit. "I'm prepared to take you on as a student if you follow three disciplines: no-smoking, celibacy and vegetarianism," he said in response. I was a bit shocked by the starkness of this offer. I had never contemplated a life with any of these disciplines. And I had no way of knowing what he was offering in exchange. I weighed it up quickly in my mind. There was nothing else I wanted to do with my life at that juncture and I could always drop out if the going got tough.

"OK", I agreed. I don't remember how the conversation went from there. It was forty-two years ago when I was a mere twenty-six years old. I do however remember him encouraging me to buy a book from Foyle's bookshop in Tottenham Court Road. Despite being reminded several times I resisted this suggestion for a couple of months as an act of defiance. I wanted to prove to myself that I was still capable of choosing my own path (in the East this would be interpreted as ego resistance). Several months later I decided that it was now safe for me to make the journey to Foyle's bookshop. But when I got there who was waiting at the door but Kamal!

It was mid-winter and freezing cold. Not exactly the weather to be hanging about in the street. "What are you doing here?" I asked. "Waiting for you" came the reply. I quickly ran different scenarios through my head. Perhaps someone told him I was coming today? But no one else knew I was making this purchase on this particular day. Perhaps he had been waiting every day for just this opportunity? I dismissed this as extremely unlikely especially deep into the cold of winter. "I'm here to buy that book you wanted me to get," I added, still slightly shocked to see him. "Come, I'll buy it for you," he replied. This was getting weird!

If Kamal really did know what would happen before the event what did that mean for the nature of our reality? Was the future predestined? And what did it say about freedom of choice? Were we just acting out a script that had already been written? I had a lot of internal questioning going on but I was careful not to come to any conclusion without further investigation.

The book he had recommended was "The Autobiography of a Yogi" by Paramahansa Yogananda. The book turned out to be very interesting, listing a whole series of alleged 'occult powers' which presented me with more possible evidence of phenomena which were completely outside my current world-view. This was an area I definitely wanted to explore and, in Kamal, I had found someone who appeared to be the perfect guide.

It was now becoming clear to my housemates that I had

been seduced by the false promises of religion. A fallen comrade! To be honest, I was quite surprised myself at the leap of faith I had made. I thought it best to part company with my housemates, while we were still on civil terms, by finding alternative accommodation as soon as I possibly could. Fortunately, a flat was being advertised further up Ladbroke Grove, towards the 'posh' end at Notting Hill. There were houses there that reminded me of wedding cake, long rows of identical white, terraced flats. A thin wall separated me from my neighbour on the top floor. Creaky floorboards revealed their every movement although I never actually saw them. The flat was within easy walking distance of Kamal's flat which was my main concern.

As our chats progressed, I learned that Kamal claimed to have little glass beads manifesting on his mantelpiece. He claimed to be able to interpret from these beads a set of instructions from his guru. Now I was well outside my comfort zone. If what Kamal claimed was true, there was a whole dimension out there about which I knew nothing and, more to the point, my entire belief system would have been stood on its head!

Kamal and I were considering the general topic of karma over a cup of coffee. He took a large gulp and immediately spat something out into his hand. He was sitting opposite me, about a metre away, so I had an excellent view of the situation. It looked triangular in shape but it wasn't clear what it was till he stuck out his tongue.

His tongue was missing a central "v" shape and now looked a bit like a snake's tongue. Immediately he put his hand to his ear (he claimed to be clairaudient, that is, to hear the voice of his guru, which raised several more questions in my mind). We had been discussing references to karma contained in Yogananda's book, a topic about which I was still unsure. I couldn't get past the idea of a little accountant sitting up there keeping a tally of our pros and cons. Anyway, Kamal's reaction was to look straight over to me immediately after the event and say, as best he could with half his tongue missing, that it was a live illustration of how karma works "for your benefit!"

As I said before, I felt my relationship with Kamal had now progressed to the point where he wouldn't try to con me. There could be no doubt about it as there in his hands lay a section of his tongue. This was quite a moment for me. This was the first time I had actually witnessed something that was outside my understanding of the world. By this time, I had read plenty of accounts of strange goings-on but to witness it first-hand for the first time was a pretty important stage in my development. Before, I would have dismissed the notion of a spiritual realm as hocus-pocus and seen the Kamal incident as a staged event. But now I was having to rethink my mental model of the world. Perhaps I had been wrong all these years. I suppose for you, the reader this will be a written account of strange goings-on so you in turn will have to judge its veracity for yourself.

Over the next couple of months, we discussed many aspects of the spirit world. I was totally amazed that there was another reality out there about which I had been completely unaware. Then one day I bumped into Kamal's next-door neighbour whom I knew, in the street, and was informed that Kamal had been taken into hospital with leukaemia. I had no knowledge of this disease at the time but a short while later I made my way to the hospital ward where he was being treated. He was very pleased to see me as he had become very confused. In particular he was concerned that they might be tampering with his food in order to increase his protein levels. He feared they might be disguising egg yolk in his orange juice and thus giving him food that was outside the boundaries of his strict vegetarian diet. Little did I know that, many years later, I too would come to know this same hospitalised confusion.

A few days after this visit I bumped into one of his neighbours who informed me, much to my amazement, that Kamal had subsequently passed on. I use the expression passed on intentionally, because I have no doubts about the fact that he simply shed one body to inhabit another. In fact, after my initial shock, I remember laughing because 'going beyond' the physical had always been one of Kamal's main ambitions. He seemed to have achieved that much sooner than we all expected. I buried Kamal after a Christian funeral simply because I didn't know who else to contact. It was a very small funeral, especially for someone who had played such an important role in my life, but I had no details of any other contacts and I knew that he certainly wouldn't have wanted a Muslim funeral. In the total absence of any details of his family I phoned the Egyptian embassy in London and asked them to pursue the matter. In the absence of Kamal I decided to move into his flat to 'keep his flag flying' by continuing the meditative lifestyle that Kamal had shown me.

After his burial I did trace one of Kamal's contacts in London, which suggested that there were probably other contacts and possibly friends of Kamal in London who might never know what happened to him. The one contact I did know about was a trainee priest who had been told to stop indulging in occult matters but who had been party to Kamal's psychic exploits in the past. Let's call him Andrew. Andrew met me at Kamal's flat. He verified Kamal's glass bead stories claiming that he had been present at the time. He seemed totally genuine so I had no reason to doubt his account which in many ways was quite troubling because the evidence of some strange new reality was mounting up. It was no longer something I could ignore. I never saw any beads in Kamal's flat but I personally have no doubt about the veracity of their accounts.

I wasn't sure what to do with Kamal's personal property so I asked Andrew if there were any items that he wanted to take away as mementos of Kamal. He replied that there was nothing that he wanted "except perhaps a shilling that Kamal had touched." No sooner had he said this, than he put his hand to his ear in much the same way that Kamal used to. But this time the clairaudient message was allegedly from Kamal. 'Look inside the suit pocket,' came the message. We did this but there was nothing to be found. My doubts started to re-emerge. Perhaps all this was an elaborate game! What else could the message have meant? There was only one suit and the pockets had been searched. In desperation I searched the pockets again. Still nothing, "But wait, there's a hole in the lining of the pocket". My hand reached down and there in the material below the pocket was a coin. When we eventually fished it out, we found it was an old shilling coin. We stared at each other quizzically. What could it mean? Then we remembered Andrew's words about wanting only a shilling that Kamal had touched. Well, we had our shilling! Spooky or what? Andrew then departed and I never saw him again.

I wasn't sure what the next step was for me in order to get some sense of direction back in my life after Kamal's sudden departure. By now I was well into the idea that psychic messages would reveal the way forward. Visiting a psychic is not something that I had done before, or indeed since. Neither is it something that I would recommend to anyone. I suppose it's an interesting experience but you can never be sure who is handing out the advice or how reliable it is. Anyway, I decided to visit a place that I'd heard Kamal refer to, the Spiritualist Association. At the time I was not able to distinguish between psychic phenomena and spirituality so attending a clairvoyant session seemed a perfectly reasonable way of taking forward my own spiritual development.

The Spiritualist Association was housed in an odd building, set in the impressive Russell Square, in Central London. Inside, it was very grand and over four stories high. It had once been a stylish Edwardian property. And talking of Edwardian things, one lady in her early thirties I would guess, was dressed completely in a black Edwardian costume topped by a black hat, and with a black parasol in her hand. She claimed to remember her last birth and the address at which she had previously lived. Her Edwardian personality had become so real for her that she had apparently chosen to sacrifice her 20th century personality in order to live out this strange Edwardian identity. This seemed an odd decision to me but it was yet another thought-provoking experience.

I discovered that one of the mediums 'performing' that day was a woman who had worked with Kamal in some context. I thought that might be a useful place to start so I joined her session in a group of about thirty. I remember that the Edwardian lady was in the session. About half the way through the session, a session mainly comprising of family politics and possessions, the medium turned to me, sending the blood racing through my veins. "I want to come to you sir. I've got a gentleman here who passed very recently with pain in his throat." I noticed that she didn't identify Kamal. She continued, "He wants to thank you for following him, especially as you're more advanced than him, and you knew it." That came as a bit of a shock! The bit about following him was uncannily accurate though, and quite different in tone to all the other messages in that session.

"He's showing me a red brick building and he says, 'don't waste your time'." The only red brick building I could think of was the cafe in which I regularly took my lunch. It was true that I had been making friends with the pretty Italian waitress in there. Could that be the reference? Had the disembodied soul of Kamal been spying on me? I searched around for other explanations. I couldn't find any. My lunchtime arrangements changed from that day on.

Then finally: "He's showing me a big sunset and is saying, 'don't worry, you'll get there with another group'." I didn't know what this last bit was about, but in view of my recent experiences, I was more inclined to give credence to all this than I would have been just a few months previously. Only recently did I make the connection with a mountain top called Sunset Point, where I later used to meditate, high in the mountains of Rajasthan in India.

From my trip to the Spiritualist Association I concluded two things: I needed to find some sort of group that might 'get me there' wherever 'there' was! Secondly, I came across the name of the Ramakrishna Vedanta Centre which was located in nearby Holland Park. I had read a lot about Sri Ramakrishna in the book which Kamal had recommended. From his photo it was clear that he was a true renunciant which appealed to the remnant of my socialist values.

Vedanta is a philosophy based on the teachings of the Upanishads, one of India's key religious texts. There are three central principles: 1. A single universal consciousness, 2. The divinity of the soul and 3. The equal validity of all religions.

The idea of universal 'mind' appealed to me. As Burns put it 'A man's a man for a' that.' There was something quite attractive to me about a shared consciousness. And the idea that there was a thing called a soul that transcended one single birth, especially after 'Edwardian lady,' opened up all sorts of possibilities for me. The notion that the soul is 'divine' also sat comfortably with me by this stage of my experience. The idea that there was a 'God' in every man and woman was quite in line with my previous political beliefs.

The Ramakrishna Vedanta Centre turned out to be located on 'Millionaire's Row.' The Holland Park area, I discovered, was comprised of some very big, detached mansions all painted a lemon shade that distinguished them from the other big mansions around central London. It was clear that Sri Ramakrishna was now moving in some pretty elevated circles; I decided to put my prejudice aside. My personal need for spiritual company took precedence at the time.

I went along to one of their Sunday gatherings. And

yes, it did feel much better to be part of a gathering of like-minded souls. Inside, it was what an estate agent might describe as 'well-appointed.' Outside the main room there was a small 'ante room,' in which sat a small bowl of cold water. Unfortunately, I found myself at the front of a small queue and it suddenly occurred to me that this might be the holy water that had been mentioned several times in the book Kamal had recommended.

I was conscious of the other members of the short queue, all Asian men, looking at me curiously to see what I was doing. The stakes were high. I needed to make a decision on my next move, one that wouldn't offend my new companions. I cupped my hands together, then poured some of the water carefully into my mouth before disposing of most of it surreptitiously over my head, finishing as per the text-books by rubbing my two hands dutifully on my head. If this was indeed holy water I had surely performed impressively in front of my new acquaintances. I then lingered to see if the others would follow in my footsteps but, to my horror, they washed their hands in the bowl saying nothing about what must have seemed like my very eccentric behaviour. Maybe they thought all non-Indians were weird. Or perhaps they thought it was an act of supreme humility! Maybe not.

Once through the ante-room, I arrived at the main meeting room. There were about 40 adults sitting cross-legged on the floor, a large garlanded portrait of Sri Ramakrishna sat at the very front of the room. This time

I decided to wait by the door for the others to show me what was what. After they entered the room each in turn prostrated in front of the garlanded photo of Sri Ramakrishna then turned before joining the back of the gathering. I duly followed their example.

The Sunday sessions at that time consisted of a talk by the resident Swami who appeared to be well-fed unlike Sri Ramakrishna himself. This was followed by the singing of some bhajans. The equivalent to Christian hymns. The Swami was assisted by a young Englishman, who could have been a Roman Catholic altar boy in other circumstances. Whereas the Swami was distant and remote, doubtless busy reciting his mantra, the younger man engaged freely with the participants at the end of the proceedings.

I had a definite feeling of belonging to the group and felt comfortable with each of the central planks of Vedanta, that all of the world's religions were equally valid, a sentiment that appealed to my politics. The main problem was that while Sri Ramakrishna himself may have enjoyed 'samadhi' or universal consciousness, the rest of us were left hoping that some miracle might happen. George Harrison perhaps best described the frustration of the situation: "I really want to see you Lord, but it takes so long I know".

It was exasperating too to simply sit there, week after week, waiting for a crumb to fall from the master's table.

I was later to visit shrines across India, and noticed that, no matter where I went, there was this same mixture of hope and impatience. In rural parts of India and in the smaller towns such places were used primarily as venues for social gatherings and for groups to practice bonding rituals. I never got the impression that there was any significant spiritual development going on apart from the Swamis and a small core of devout followers who appeared to be intensely engrossed in the various rituals.

There's not much more I remember of this time; I once made an appointment with the swami to discuss ways of deepening my meditation. "Play a little music when you meditate," came the reply. Not the deep insight I was hungering for. I didn't feel that I was making much progress, when compared to my time with Kamal.

Bhakti Yoga, that is to say devotional yoga, where songs are sung and rituals performed, is one of four main paths of yoga contained within Hinduism, the others being Gyan Yoga, mastery of the scriptures, Hatha Yoga, the most popular yoga in the West, comprised of a range of physical postures. And finally, Raja Yoga, concerned with mind control and meditation.

The Ramkrishna Centre, which was based on Bhakti Yoga, left me feeling better but not any wiser. Although there was some meditation it was difficult to experience any emotion as we strived towards 'universal consciousness'. Sri Ramakrishna appeared to be deep in bliss in his state of samadhi but the image made me more frustrated than ever.

It was against this background that I decided to drop in to a Raja Yoga exhibition which was taking place just 200 metres from my flat. I was with an old university chum who was visiting for the day and we casually strolled around the exhibition which was comprised of a collection of Indian illustrations. We were not overly impressed by the philosophy depicted in the pictures which appeared quite simplistic to our 'sophisticated' Western minds. As we subtly made our way to the exit, we were told that a meditation was about to start, "Would you like to stay, it will only take a few minutes?" Since it was an Indian lady who did the asking, we decided to do our bit for race relations and stay back for a few minutes. Neither of us were particularly moved by the meditation and left feeling a bit mystified about what we had just experienced.

A few hours later I arrived back at my flat. That was when I noticed that something highly significant had changed. Deep inside there was a profound sense of peace. For someone who had been through some unsettling experiences recently, like the trauma of Kamal's sudden disappearance, my unexpected change of direction, exam finals, this came as a welcome, but totally unexpected development. If I had been searching for something, then this was it! Above all I was intrigued by how the transformation had taken place. I was especially interested in how such a profound change had occurred. I had not done anything unusual except attending that exhibition. It seemed the most likely source of this remarkable experience was my time at the exhibition. Needless to say, I thought at the time that I could never accept their worldview but I was keen to experience more of their company, the effect of which I couldn't deny, was extremely powerful.

And so, another chapter was about to unfold. With the intention of spending a bit more time in their company in order to explore this weird power, I rang the number advertised on their leaflet that I had picked up at the exhibition and spoke to an Indian woman who steered me towards attending a free seven-day course. It wasn't exactly what I was looking for as I had no strong appetite for more dubious philosophy. It was the company of these mysterious teachers that I sought. I thought that visiting their Centre might open up some opportunities to drink the amazing nectar that these Raja Yogis seemed to possess.

CHAPTER 4. RAJA YOGA

The Centre was located in Kilburn, formerly famous as a predominantly Irish enclave but now home to a mostly black population. It was comprised of two small terraced houses, a stark difference to the Sri Ramakrishna Centre that I'd grown used to. In actual fact, this Centre struck me as more authentic and much more in line with my values.

A young American woman dressed in a white sari gave me my first lesson. I was a bit alarmed when I saw the sari. Had I stumbled into a cult? Was this another Hare Krishna type outfit? The theme of the first class was 'The Soul'. Was I a body with a soul or a soul with a body? It was quite thought-provoking. Which was the real me? According to what I was being taught, I the soul am an eternal being of light. That word eternal is important, she explained, because it meant that there has never been a time when I was not me. And that was important because any self-development would reap rewards not just in this birth, but in the future too. I asked a question that I thought might wrong-foot her. "How come the population of the world is increasing, if the soul is eternal?

Without hesitation, she explained to me there is a 'soul bank' where souls reside until their part in the drama unfolds. Thus, over time more and more souls are joining the drama. Now, some of this I had previously come across in my reading. But the interesting new twist for me was that the purpose given for the yoga meditation was to enter a state where all this became a real experience and not just a belief; which is the buffer I had hit at the Sri Ramakrishna Centre.

I ran all this through for myself. If I am a soul, then the identity of the body, Stuart Hepburn, is just the name of the part I am playing. When the body of Stuart Hepburn eventually dies, as it must, I will no longer be in this body and will take on a new identity. It was an interesting proposition, and the Edwardian lady from the Spiritualist Association crossed my mind as I mulled over the lesson. The 'existential angst' that we tend to carry, because we know deep down that we are destined to die sooner or later, falls away if I consider myself as a transcendent being. But is that just wishful thinking? My recent experiences challenged old prejudices and beliefs that had become redundant in the face of all that I'd been through in recent months.

One thing she mentioned especially grabbed my attention. It was about relationships. "It is the soul that yearns for love yet we repeatedly get involved in physical relationships that never satisfy the soul. After repeating the pattern numerous times, the soul becomes weak and tired. In meditation the soul can experience the spiritual love it craves."

There were other parts of the course that I found less easy to accept but I decided just to park any doubts alongside my other concerns and continue with the amazing meditations. On my way out of the Centre after the very first lesson I bumped into a tiny figure, an Indian lady in her sixties. She was followed by an equally small lady, possibly late twenties, early thirties. The older lady (who I later learned was the senior teacher at the Centre) said, in Hindi without prompting, "I recognise you. You can come to 4am meditation tomorrow morning". The younger lady, who I'll call "Ninabhen" to protect her identity, translated into English for me.

Instantly I weighed up this exchange. Maybe she said that to everyone? Maybe she had been waiting for me to come out of the room! Yet she said it as though it was a great privilege she was bestowing! I decided to make my way home and consider it rationally. But on thinking about it, the prospect of another dose of that meditation nectar loomed large in my imagination and eventually it became a no-brainer. Of course, I was going to the 4am meditation.

To my surprise the little meditation room was packed at

4 a.m. next morning. About half the attendees were of Indian origin, but what surprised me most was that the other half were westerners. I managed to find a space where I sat cross-legged on the floor. And the meditation didn't disappoint. My consciousness floated away like a helium balloon. From that day on 4am meditation at the Centre became a regular event.

My lessons also continued although at this stage I was much more attracted by the meditation than the philosophy. In fact, there were bits, like the circularity of time or the predestined nature of events, that I found hard to accept. But all obstacles were simply parked. I felt that my head was full of ideas and beliefs I had drawn from books but which had got me nowhere. Now I was going somewhere. I certainly didn't want book-learning to get in the way.

I noticed that everyone at the Centre was "glowing", surrounded by an aura of white light, and I wondered how it could be possible for the entire group to be affected in this way. I came to the conclusion that the senior teacher must be a very powerful yogi to have generated so much power. I finished the course and nodded politely at the bits I found most difficult to accept.

According to the teachings that I had received on the course, God was not omnipresent but a single detached being of light. If God was omnipresent, the argument went, it would be a case of God looking for God. It was also pointed out that an omnipresent God would be present in the form of a cesspit. And there was another intriguing notion mentioned: that God is not the giver of sorrow and happiness. What was being suggested was that God was a purely benevolent being and that any sad situations were a product of our own karma. This was a very different take on God from the one I had imagined during my childhood.

One other idea interested me, once again on the topic of relationships. The teacher mentioned that the aim of Raja Yoga meditation was to have a 'relationship' with God, like that of a child to its parent. This, she assured me, would not just be a devotional relationship but one in which the parent would play an active part in the meditation. I already had experience of something being 'done' to me during meditation so that didn't come as a surprise, but it was fascinating nevertheless.

I could cope with most of what I'd heard, although the notion that there was an entity called "God" who was not omnipresent ran contrary to everything I had read in my Eastern books. And the notion that the teacher presented of time being circular, with a constantly repeating drama, was pretty mind blowing and not a notion that fitted well into my intellect. But I couldn't deny the power I felt in meditation. Once again, I decided to park my doubts and just continue with the blissful meditations. It felt like my book-learning was pulling me in one direction, but here I was transcending all that learning and experiencing something completely new, something I'd only dreamt of before.

And so, I started to apply some of the ideas I had been taught and became an effort-making yogi. I was very happy to have arrived in such a pleasant, you could almost say loving, group of people. I continued to check for any signs of cult status, but there were none and I was impressed by the general intelligence in the room. These were not a collection of 'lost souls' or strays shepherded together by a charismatic leader for mutual support. These were powerful individuals making rational choices about the direction that their lives should take.

At some point, I can't remember when, the matter of celibacy was raised. It was a key feature of life as a Raja Yogi apparently. It was not an issue for me since I had already been on that path with Kamal. I had never really considered it to be a life-long commitment though, merely a transitional phase, a discipline that I was quite prepared to follow in order to acquire more knowledge and absorb more of this amazing nectar.

Eventually, I was invited to teach a new student. I suppose that by this time I had enough faith to perform quite well in the teaching role, although at some level I was still wrestling with the idea of an ever-repeating drama. But I was about to experience something truly amazing and by this time my threshold for amazing was pretty high. I had just finished teaching one of these introductory sessions and as usual we closed with a meditation. I sat opposite the young man meditating with eyes open when suddenly without warning, 'a thunderbolt' surged through my body. Its power was unlike anything I'd experienced before. But what was truly amazing was that the power came bang on cue. Was I being used as an instrument to give another soul an experience?

For the very first time the thought crossed my mind that I could dedicate my life to being an instrument for this amazing energy. I considered lots of possibilities. By now I had become comfortable talking about God. Could this surge of power really be connected with God? I had always thought of God as a historical entity, who was said to have shown Himself (or Herself) only briefly in the Bible, thousands of years ago. It was still a shock to me that he, she, or it, might be a sentient being in 'real time'.

What I knew was that some energy had passed through me, bang on cue. As yet I had no evidence that it was an energy for good or bad, let alone Divine! But it set me thinking. Maybe it wasn't the teachers who were powerful. Maybe, as they claimed, it was simply energy passing through them. Maybe, as they had said, there was a non-physical being behind all this. Maybe, as they claimed, it was the entity known as God! I realise that readers will have their own interpretations of all this, given their own different beliefs and prejudices.

I satisfied myself about the benevolence of the energy I was working with and the reassuring emphasis that was laid on honesty in all settings. In meditation I had an experience, some would say vision, of an atomic explosion that was much less powerful than I was in my stage of soul consciousness. The prospect of nuclear war was not new to me. It had seemed fairly likely that, sooner or later, some psychopath would get their hands on a nuclear weapon.

Climate change and international tensions were notions I had long anticipated. It seemed that the Centre's teachers also expected things to get worse before they got better. But this was a very positive development for me, for the idea that there could be light at the end of a very dark tunnel was completely new to me (at the time of writing, Donald Trump was rattling the cage of Kim Jong-Un, and nuclear war seemed a very real possibility).

An interesting scenario developed not long after I had started going to the Centre. A large group of black youths, maybe a hundred strong, had gathered outside the building. It was a time when black youths used to want to fight with the recently arrived (from Uganda) Pakistanis. Mistaking the Centre as a place where 'Pakis' gathered, they congregated outside in a hostile manner. It looked at one stage that they might attack the Centre.

There were about five Westerners in the Centre at the

time and we quickly discussed how to handle the issue. We agreed that it would possibly defuse the situation if we showed the crowd that this was more than just a houseful of 'Pakis.' So, we went outside and stood stock-still in meditation. It was the first real test of my ability to stay in soul-consciousness. The Scottish muscles in my body yearned to dive aggressively into the crowd and my meditation only just held me back. It was my first major success in conquering the dictates of my body. After shouts of "Paki-lovers" the crowd eventually dispersed.

However, the first major wobble of my new life as a Raja Yogi came not long after, when I was storing a piece of equipment in a shed at the Yoga Centre. Ninabhen was passing by and shouted jokingly "I hope you are still around to dig that out next year!" Perhaps curiously, it had never occurred to me that I might not be around the Centre in a year's time. I had had the feeling that I'd arrived at my final destination and that others, especially the teachers, knew that; especially after the senior teacher's initial 'endorsement.' But now, suddenly, I started to think about where else I might be in a year's time.

At that time, I wasn't sufficiently advanced to take responsibility for my own confusion so, internally in a very subtle way, I blamed Ninabhen for my confusion; and in so doing started down a path that would have serious consequences in the years to come. Perhaps for the first time, I experienced spiritual 'vertigo,' the feeling that I might fall from this very comfortable place. I was rattled.

No more bliss-full meditation for me, her words reverberated in my meditations. Unbeknown to me at the time, my focus switched from spiritual growth to spiritual survival.

A short time after this Ninabhen said, again lightheartedly, "There's going to be fun and games when your old patterns emerge," I immediately felt as though I was wearing a suicide vest that could explode at any second. That when I least expected it some of my old beliefs and behaviours would burst out of me, not unlike the Incredible Hulk. Rather than thinking of myself as a bit unstable in my yogic stage it was again easier to locate blame outside myself and Ninabhen was the obvious target.

Rather than remaining introverted to address the fact that I had allowed my attention to wander, I began to see a deliberate pattern of undermining. It had not gone unnoticed that the teachers were exclusively female and I dare say there was more than a modicum of male ego on display at this time, (indeed, later too!). My relationship with Ninabhen began to deteriorate rapidly as I held her accountable for my meltdown. It was of course my own instability that was the problem but it was to take several decades for me to grasp this point.

At the time, I was concerned that my attention was being repeatedly drawn to her words and I didn't acknowledge the resentment that was kindling inside me at finding myself knocked off my very comfortable perch. I remember commenting around this time that I had not been angry since coming to the Centre. What I meant of course was that I had not expressed anger since coming to the Centre. Was it attachment that was drawing my mind repeatedly to these comments? All I could be sure of was that I found the going much harder from this point on. After a very promising start things were to get more complicated now. Initially I had been given the nickname 'Surrendra' because of my willingness to surrender myself to the Raja Yoga disciplines. But that nickname was abandoned in the light of more recent developments.

I had never chosen the path of celibacy as a lifestyle choice. Celibacy had always been a way of getting access to learning. And now it seemed like a commitment that I was being asked to make for the long term. I wasn't sure how I felt about that. Circumstances had enabled me to drift into this scenario and now the full implications of my present situation began to dawn on me. But at the same time, I also knew that I had found everything that I'd been looking for. Walking away now was not an option. If celibacy was the price I had to pay, so be it!

Above all, there was still immense excitement at how quickly my life had been completely turned around and now I desired to take all of this back to my native Scotland. It really concerned me that no one in Scotland had had the opportunity to have this experience.

And so, it was that after just a few months in the London Centre I set off for Edinburgh, my former home. The intention was to open a Centre in Edinburgh. For the initial period, I was accompanied by a fellow student from London. But he left, and I forged ahead on my own, heavily reliant on my meditation to keep me on track. It was probably during this time that I first got used to the idea of solitary meditation, an experience that was later to play such a big part in my life.

Eventually I obtained a rented flat and, somewhat to my surprise, a teacher from the London Centre travelled up and took over both the flat and my public speaking commitments in Edinburgh and Glasgow. I suppose I had imagined myself in the lead role by virtue of the fact that there was no other option and I also had doubts about how successful a London teacher would be in a Scottish environment but I quickly adjusted to the role of facilitator for our service in Scotland. We rapidly grew a class of eight regular attendees. Everything was progressing well enough in Edinburgh so I felt comfortable leaving everything behind and setting off for my first visit to the spiritual headquarters in India. At a conscious level, I was going to deepen my faith but as I look back now I can recognise that the Scottish trait of checking things out for authenticity was also a part of my agenda. If there was a cult to be found I would find it!

Our flight landed in Bombay (or Mumbai, as it is now known.) As we stepped out of the aircraft door I was hit immediately by the essence of India. The rays of a burning hot sun and the curious mixture of animal dung, incense and freshly cooked spicy food. There was also the constant hooting of passing vehicles. It was a sensory blast that stirred me from the stupor of a seventeen-hour flight. The airport terminal was a hive of activity, not unlike an ants' nest. The terminal was packed with people largely dressed in white pyjamas, all travelling in different directions and, apparently, all talking as they did so.

Once through the terminal, the excitement continued with my first journey in a Tuk-tuk taxi. A very small yellow and black three-wheeler, always driven by a man with a towel wrapped round his head and, judging by his driving, over his eyes too. When we reached our destination, a low-lying, white, concrete building we were met by a reception committee of teachers dressed in the usual white saris, who told the driver in no uncertain terms that he was overcharging us. In typical Indian fashion taxi drivers appeared from all directions to support their beleaguered colleague and the situation turned into a noisy melee. But there was no doubt who was going to win the argument and our taxi charges were slashed accordingly.

In the Centre, we got our first taste of what it would be like to live in a big city like Bombay. Outside in the busy street there was a continuous wail of vehicle horns which seemed to be a standard feature of Indian driving and there was the continuous roar of 50cc scooters often carrying whole families and even the odd animal. The rooms of the Centre were primarily functional with large open spaces suitable for meditation and minimum decor on the white walls. On a balcony at the rear and sheltered from the traffic noise several old ladies, also dressed in white saris, squatted on the ground beside a small gas cylinder and some very wide pans, evidently preparing food for their newly arrived and frankly very hungry guests. By now I was used to eating in silence using my hands. We all sat cross-legged on the concrete floor upon which a brightly coloured sheet had been laid. The food, which was also familiar to me, was well-cooked and very welcome after the long flight during which we had survived on cold samosas.

After an uneventful night in a local hotel a small group of us were invited to go to the Indian Prime Minister's official residence to meet with Mr. Desai, the Indian Prime Minister at the time. A former student of Mahatma Gandhi, he was as self-aware as you would expect asking us not to pin a badge on his Nehru jacket, the traditional woollen jacket of choice in India, but to use the button hole instead. 'Why make a hole needlessly?' I'm not sure whether this level of reflection made for an effective international statesman but it was quite impressive to me at the time. Certainly, in 1977 I didn't realise how fortunate I was to be involved in this meeting with the leader of the world's largest democracy. But I do now!

With the Indian Prime Minister, Mr. Moraji Desai in 1977. (I am standing behind the Indian lady).

We took part in a long procession through the streets of Bombay and attended a three-day conference, about which I'm afraid I remember nothing, then we boarded a train for a three-day journey, largely through the sandy desert of Rajasthan. The train journey was intriguing with animals in the train's corridor seated beside some young boys who were staring curiously at our every move. As we rolled into the numerous stations, even in the middle of the night, we were met by calls of "garam chai" (hot tea), and arms were extended through the window rails, usually by mothers holding small babies, pleading very desperately for buck-sheesh (small change).

Poverty was all around us. There were whole families camped out on the railway platforms and there were even makeshift homes at the sides of the rail track. It was difficult to witness this degree of poverty, although I dare say it was even more difficult for these families to endure it! We could see right into their flimsy homes. They were completely empty of possessions save perhaps for a single cooking utensil. This was a scene that was to feature in all of our experiences in the populated areas of India. We slept on thinnish benches that folded down from the carriage wall. I don't remember there being any bedding but I slept right through till 4 a.m. meditation next morning. At the time it never occurred to me to wonder how the young boys in the corridor had managed to sleep.

Occasionally, from the train we'd come across a lone female figure apparently in the middle of the desert, with no civilisation to be seen, collecting the very few twigs and branches that were scattered across the desert floor. And on their heads would be a stack of their previous collections. Which raised the questions where had they come from and what were they doing out here in the middle of nowhere?

After three days' travel, we finally arrived at the hill-station of Mount Abu, our destination. A hill-station is a place high in the mountains to which the British Raj used to retreat from the full onslaught of the fierce summer sun that blasted the cities below. The central feature of the town was a very large polo field, still used, but now by

Indians mimicking their former Imperial rulers on thin, bony, little Indian horses.

The ashram where we were to stay was comprised of a collection of immaculately whitewashed buildings. One new block had been built especially for us foreigners. We were mainly from London but there were a handful of Australians and a few Americans together with a few individuals from Central and Southern America. The residents of the ashram seemed genuinely delighted to see us and during the course of our stay showed us what it meant to be a Raja Yogi. They would move around with focused minds, catering for our every need and seeming to thoroughly enjoy our presence. The senior teachers too were able to answer our questions.

At a conscious level, I was completely on board with everything, but as I look back, I now see that there was a little part of me looking out for any cracks in the organisation that would indicate that something untoward was going on behind the scenes, and that this was really a scam. But, search as I could, all seemed to be genuine. The closest I could get to a scandal was when the senior teacher clouted me heavily round the back of the neck while we were fooling about. I probably deserved a clout but it still came as quite a shock in that setting. Apparently, that sort of reprimand was normal in India. The senior teachers worked even harder than the rest and usually got by on just two hours sleep! They were leading by example.

Sometimes some of the local men would carry a large carpet for us so as to have 'picnics' close to the ashram. Armies of monkeys, sometimes 50 strong, and bold as brass, would approach us in an intimidating manner and I would channel my old warrior self and launch myself into their midst. At the time it felt like fun, but with hindsight it was a fairly aggressive part of my ashram visit. We would rise at 3.30 a.m. and gather in the meditation hall at 4 a.m. At that time the hall could hold 1000 of us which felt pretty awesome (the newest hall now holds 30,000 so you can imagine how that feels.)

Whereas my concept of yogic life had been a fairly harsh one of effort and renunciation I learned from the locals that there was another side to Raja Yoga that was about generosity and 'royal bearing.' The ashram residents were all friendly and helpful although I wasn't too keen on the rigid separation of males and females even in the classroom, a cultural tradition in India which, to my mind, intensifies the polarity between the two. I even tried to address my problem with Ninabhen as I had felt this tension was damaging to my meditation. Her words had been the source of so much heartache for me that I began to wonder if this was some sort of karmic account being settled. But my approach was dismissed in no uncertain fashion. The problem was laid squarely at the feet of my troublesome old patterns.

We would meditate from 4 till 5 a.m., shower, then start morning class at 6 a.m. After morning class, we would have breakfast around 8.30 a.m. Unbeknown to us foreigners there was a tradition in the ashram that those serving food would continue offering food until their guests were fully satisfied and only then would they eat from whatever food remained. Hungry Westerners, unaware of this tradition, couldn't believe their luck when an apparently endless supply of food was offered to them. The young Columbian lad next to me was on his fifth round of jam and chapatis. Needless to say, it took only a few days of this over-consumption for a resource problem to emerge and it was explained to us that just because an unlimited amount of food was offered it didn't mean we had to accept. The kitchen staff were apparently going without as a result of our over-indulgence. Another feature of yogic life fell into place: self-control in all situations!

While we were in the ashram a fair proportion of the Westerners fell sick. We received a lecture about the need to strengthen our ability to fight off disease and I remember reacting to this: "What can we do? Our bodies simply aren't used to the local bacteria". At the time, and probably for a good few years later, I had no notion of the mind-body relationship that was possible in Raja Yoga. It was a long time later that I finally grasped the creator/creation relationship of the soul and body.

This same problem arose on the day that we finally took our leave from Mount Abu. The road down the mountain involved numerous loops and, together with the drop in air pressure, left me feeling completely washed out by the time we got to the bottom of the hill. When the train finally arrived at the station I climbed aboard and collapsed into a fold-down bed feeling dreadful. An Indian teacher immediately pounced. "What sort of example are you setting?" I didn't feel there was much choice at the time and felt a bit harassed. It was only many years later that the mind-body relationship practiced in Raja Yoga began to dawn on me.

I don't remember much more of that trip, and strangely, none of the next trip, which started in Delhi and saw a party from Scotland travel for the first time. They were to be introduced as part of the London group, which seemed an odd decision, and one that was to have unfortunate consequences further down the line.

And so, to the final trip in 1979, about which I remember quite a lot. I think there were only three or four of us on the Air Afghanistan flight which stopped off in Kabul. I've written extensively about this trip in "A Most Curious Detour," so I'll just summarise the highlights of the trip for the benefit of those who haven't read that book. It was such a key part of my story that I don't mind taking the risk of being seen to repeat myself.

Stepping out of the plane in Kabul was like stepping into a furnace. That was the first indication that we were deep in Asia. As we waited in the airport for the plane to be serviced, we sat in a big room that served as a lounge. All around the walls there were large photos of members of the government who looked, to my eyes, like a collection of pantomime villains. It was a relief to fly out of there and from the plane we could see the poverty and harshness of Afghan life etched out in the mud houses below and the bleak brown landscapes.

Our next destination was Delhi Airport, less chaotic than Bombay, yet still very busy. As usual the porters tussled for the opportunity to carry our luggage and potentially earn an inflated tip. This time we headed straight for the train which would take us to Rajasthan in three days and to our final destination Mount Abu, in the north of India.

When we arrived at the ashram the welcome was as warm as ever and we slipped effortlessly into old relationships. As mentioned in 'A Most Curious Detour,' I was called to the gatehouse on two occasions, first to give a brief introduction to a man who was accompanied by a woman, his partner I presume, and a young child in a buggy. The man turned out to be an old Edinburgh primary school foe with whom I had wrestled many times as a small boy, He had been the 'fixer' for a gang that was widely perceived to be trouble makers and I, as leader of a band of do-gooding knights, had felt duty-bound to engage him. I was as surprised to see him as presumably he was to see me on a remote mountain top in Northern India. The way I had been taught to handle situations like this was to dissociate from my past and associate fully into my new life as a yogi. So, I welcomed them warmly to the ashram without acknowledging any shared past. It may have seemed strange to him, but hey, it worked for me!

The second meeting involved a wandering elderly American millionaire who arrived 'by chance' at the front gates. He came back a second time, emphasising his wealth, (as though that would change things), and then he vanished, no doubt in search of the next 'kick.' Following that, I can only remember leaving the ashram, (this, I think was towards the end of 1979) to embark on a prearranged lecture tour, (pictured right). This took me to a string of small towns throughout Uttar Pradesh and Madhya Pradesh as well as Rajasthan. I was impressed how the venues in each town were packed out whether it was interest in the subject matter or curiosity to see a Westerner tackle a traditionally Indian theme I would never know.

As the train trundled from town to town our small party of six was met along the route by journalists alerted by who knows whom. They were all confident individuals eager to discover some scandal hidden behind our tour. Despite their best efforts however they were not able to find the scandal that they were so desperately looking for.

Another interesting scenario took place during a visit to an Indian prison where we had received an invitation to stimulate the minds of some very bored ex-dacoits (a very large group of brigands who had terrified the Indian authorities for years, even taking on local army units). The prison itself resembled a Second World War prisoner-of-war camp with the prisoners, or at least most of them, gathered together in a large, square, open area, like a parade ground. The area was surrounded by a barbed wire topped fence manned by what looked like soldiers dressed in khaki uniforms with khaki shorts down to their knees. In their hands they appeared to be carrying old Second World War Lee Enfield rifles.

As we entered the compound a large group began to congregate in the centre, a group that mysteriously parted in the middle to permit our safe passage across the compound. We were shown onto a raised platform equipped with microphones and chairs. It felt very privileged to walk into that compound knowing that when the time came, we could simply walk back out again unlike the people round about us.

The theme of my talk that day was that, in a sense, we are all imprisoned by our body consciousness. Just as they wished they could experience the world beyond the barbed wire so we too were concerned to experience consciousness beyond the limits of the body. And so, we were all in the same boat really. In addition, their free time, together with the absence of too many distractions meant that prison might serve as quite a useful environment in which to practice mind control.

Our lecture tour took us to many small towns and it was interesting to glimpse the lives of people in small-town India. At that time, (it may have changed since), there was a surprising level of interest in spiritual matters wherever we went. People would congregate around religious shrines in the evening and it was clear that devotion played a much more central part in their lives than in the West where rationalism was well established and had more or less become the default perspective on life.

On my return to the ashram my body was exhausted and my energy depleted. Obviously, I had still not mastered the link between mind and body. As a consequence, I was admitted to the local hospital for a few days where I was treated with homeopathic medicine for the first time. It was interesting being in a medical environment where even the doctors and consultants regarded homeopathy as a legitimate treatment. I am not in a position to judge its effectiveness but I was discharged after a few days, too late however for my sister's wedding, which I had been due to attend back in Edinburgh.

Having regained my physical strength, I was ready for the 17-hour flight home, once again courtesy of Afghan Airways. The reason that this was significant is that we passed through Kabul Airport once again, this time occupied by Russian troops who had invaded Afghanistan a few weeks earlier. (We were now into 1980). There were menacing stares from what looked like crack troops and they made no pretence of the fact that their automatic weapons were trained on us. Inside the terminal there were silhouettes on the wall where the photographs of the unsavoury faces of the governing elite had once hung. They had presumably been removed by the newly arrived Russians who were no admirers of the tribal leaders.

Once safely back on board we thought the trauma was behind us until the pilot announced an unscheduled stop in Teheran. This was right in the middle of the American hostage crisis during the Iranian Cultural Revolution when the reign of the Shah of Iran was suddenly usurped by the clerical rule of Ayatollah Khomeini and friends. It was not a good time to be in Teheran! When the plane landed, we were boarded by some thinly disguised security men who, rather unconvincingly, 'cleaned the plane' and had a good look at its passengers at the same time. I guess it was some kind of snatch-squad. After the Tehran incident, we then went on to make a scheduled stop in Schiphol Airport, near Amsterdam, in Holland.

One amusing incident there I can still recall. Standing up in a gallery, I could see that the entire terminal hall was filled with turbaned heads moving restlessly around the room. There must have been an important Sikh gathering in India. Suddenly the announcer called out, "Would Mr. Singh please come to reception, that's a Mr. Singh to reception please." All of a sudden, the entire room froze and heads spun round inquisitively. Needless to say, there followed a mass surge towards the reception as all the Mr. Singhs stepped forward. It seemed that there were more than a few Mr. Singhs in the airport. And so, back to a very green and wet London.

In order to pay for my next trip to India I got a job as a courier in the City of London, working for a bank, physically moving cheques for millions of pounds around the City. It was while I was doing this that I turned the corner and bumped into the elderly US millionaire I had first met in Mount Abu, in India. To my surprise he immediately said that he had been intending to look me up in London because he was heading to South America and felt that he needed some help to get through airports. Apparently, I had come to mind.

There was something about him that I didn't entirely trust so I decided to ask the senior teacher at the Centre for guidance. She was well-known for her wise counsel and had previously been pronounced 'the most stable mind in the world' by some American university research project. She approved the trip on two conditions: firstly, that he deposited money for my return flight from the U.S. in my bank account before setting out, and secondly, that he acknowledged that I was travelling to pursue my own agenda and not his.

Within days we were touching down in Miami and heading to-wards Miami Beach where, to my shock, he chose to hire a double room in a slightly seedy hotel. I remember suggesting to the young female room cleaner who appeared at our door that she went ahead with the cleaning while I read my book. She took off like a scalded cat as though I had made an indecent proposal to her! I later understood that Miami Beach was the sort of place where no-one could be completely trusted. One very practical problem that arose from sharing a room was that I got up at 3.30 a.m. for 4 a.m. meditation and then bathed at 5 a.m. I don't think this sequence of events was much appreciated by my room-mate who I'll call Frank to conceal his real identity in this litigious world.

Frank's 'friends' in Miami more respected his status as a millionaire than liked him as a person and they let it be known, in a slightly bitter way, that he had been held in police custody for two days in relation to his wife's demise. He had of course been released uncharged because of insufficient evidence in the case but that had obviously not ended the speculation amongst his 'circle.' I could certainly recognise the potential in him to behave cruelly but it was not part of my remit to get sidetracked on this issue.

We discussed the relative merits of various South

American countries before settling on Peru for our first visit. It was clear that Frank had an American perspective on South America which was quite different to my U.K. perspective, a fact that I had not anticipated. Before long we were swapping the absurdly moist heat of summer-time Miami for the distinctly cold winter of Peru. Lima to be specific. We were both concerned to find a platform from which we could get our respective messages across. In the main street, a narrow street in the centre of town, we came across a vegetarian restaurant that was happy to host public events at short notice. I thought it would be a good idea to defer to Frank so I suggested that he spoke first and, judging from his response, that had never been in doubt.

On the day of the talks the chairs were arranged in a circle around the room and, to my surprise, they were all

The Lecture in Lima

taken by women. I wondered if spirituality was a largely feminine concern in Peru. As agreed, Frank spoke first. He outlined his plans to start a vegetarian commune somewhere in South America with babies born into a totally vegetarian environment. But to my horror he added that the project would be led "by people like Stuart".

Now this might have been a totally innocent remark but what he had done was to link me into his project as a potential leader and a potential maker of babies. Clearly some nimble footwork was required to separate the two presentations and to make it clear that I was solely concerned to promote Raja Yoga and was not part of Frank's commune. It was important to me that I maintain my own distinctive state during the presentation but I was disappointed that the waters had been muddied in this way. Anyway, I think I did succeed in separating the two in a way that was respectful to Frank's project though judging by Frank's subsequent actions I'm not sure he saw it that way.

We were both in our room later that evening when the telephone rang. Assuming it was from the desk I answered to be told that there was a small party at the desk to see Mr. Hepburn. This was quite puzzling as I was not aware of knowing anyone in Lima. When I got downstairs I recognised one of the group from the presentation. She explained that she was accompanied by her parents. Her father then did the talking and, to my amazement, he said that his daughter wanted to become my disciple and wanted me to become her guru. Now this was never going to happen as the notion of disciples and gurus was not one that I subscribed to because it was a potentially exploitative relationship. But the very prospect of such a relationship with a woman about my own age unnerved me. I can't remember exactly how I responded on the night but I remember calling a female teacher in North America next morning and suggesting that she take over the contact.

Meanwhile Frank had become upset about something I'd done. Perhaps he was still unhappy about the previous day's talks and the fact that I had not gone along with his sales pitch. The morning after our presentations while I was exploring the mountains, Frank settled the bill and set off for the airport with my return ticket to Miami in his pocket. I wasn't sure how to play this one. On the one hand I wanted to remain peaceful but on the other I felt that it was not enough to sit by passively and lose my ability to return to America. In the end I decided to take a taxi to the airport in the hope that he might still be there. And sure-enough he was, in a long queue at check-in.

Now came the next question, how to handle Frank's hissy fit? As I approached, he positively snarled with hostility. I had obviously done something that had offended him although I wasn't sure what. I searched through my experience for some guidance on how to handle the situation. The only experience that seemed remotely similar was a situation in India when we had arrived in a railway station and our luggage was disappearing in different directions in the hands of over-eager porters. One of our teachers adopted a stern demeanour and shouted out loudly in a way that restored order in an instant. That approach seemed vaguely appropriate for the current situation, or so I hoped.

I walked close to Frank and shouted out dramatically "That man has my ticket!" The sudden accusation attracted the attention of a nearby uniformed policeman whose involvement in turn sparked the attention of a senior plain-clothes officer who was keen to show off his problem-solving ability and his authority. "Is this true"? he asked Frank directly. Frank evidently didn't enjoy the attention he was currently attracting. Without replying he reached inside his jacket pocket and surrendered the ticket to the plain-clothes officer who in turn presented it to me with obvious satisfaction at his success.

I wasn't sure just what my next step would be so returned to the hotel, where my belongings were being stored, in order to think things through. Uppermost in my mind was the fact that I didn't have much money to survive without Frank's support. On balance, I decided the priority was to get back to Miami without incurring much more expense. With that in mind I decided to pack up immediately and return to the airport for the evening flight to Miami.

When I arrived back at the airport there was a long line of brightly coloured passengers waiting at the check-in, at the next desk to mine. I was later to discover that they were Cuban refugees, prisoners together with their families. They had been released from jail by a defiant Fidel Castro who was attempting to export his problem citizens to the US. For some reason this particular group had been accepted by the Peruvian government. But they had been unwilling to settle in Peru as they had clearly expressed a wish to join their compatriots in Florida.

Suddenly the long, tightly pressed line lurched forward and the plate glass window, which separated us from the tarmac, shattered and the line of refugees quickly broke through onto the airstrip. In response several police officers drew their guns with smiles of delight at the sudden prospect of a turkey shoot. Amidst the pandemonium and the gunfire my training was to freeze and slip into meditation, viewing the situation as merely another scene in the very colourful drama. It was only when I finally boarded my plane that the whole sequence of events became clear as passengers nervously unpicked the scenario. There were no casualties as far as I saw so police must have been shooting into the air.

Back in Miami it was clear that my travels with Frank had come to a sudden and unexpected end after just a few weeks. A decision was required as to what I was going to do now. A phone call to London alerted me to the fact that the Canadian Centre was about to embark on a total repaint. It was suggested that if I didn't want to cross the Atlantic yet, one option was to head up north to Toronto where there was a need for additional hands. My final pay cheque had just been paid into my account so I now had the funds to travel and Toronto seemed like a good bet.

Before long I was heading to Toronto. Almost the entire plane-full of passengers departed at Chicago and we set out for Canada with only a handful of passengers scattered throughout the 747. When we landed in Toronto it was very clear that we had crossed a border. In place of the laid-back, apparent chaos, of the Miami terminal there was the crisp starchiness of British inspired order. Neat queues and genteel politeness filled the terminal and, I'm slightly ashamed to admit, there was almost a comfortable feeling of being back in the UK.

Toronto itself proved to be a very interesting experience. As I travelled by taxi we passed through several ethnic communities, each clearly defined, and offering a variety of services peculiar to that particular ethnic culture. It was apparent that Canada was a much more diverse place than I had imagined. Yet the abundance of maple leaf flags hanging on porches was testament to the extent to which even the ethnic minorities had been successfully integrated into the host nation's identity.

When I finally arrived at the Toronto Centre it became

apparent to me that there would only be two of us to paint the whole building. Fortunately, I enjoyed decorating. Many years later I was to reflect on the contrast between decorating and the work that I was doing in human resource management, where the problem just continually changed shape. The satisfaction of looking at a painted wall at the end of the day is seldom present in HR!

Whilst in Toronto I got a call from my senior teacher in London informing me that our application for NGO (non-governmental organisation) status in the United Nations had been successful in view of our past work at the scenes of natural disasters. As a consequence, we were now eligible to attend UN conferences the first of which was in a few days' time. Would I be prepared to travel to New York and attend the conference? There was no question of me turning the opportunity down even if I was a bit uncertain of what I could add in that context.

The discussion mainly consisted of African politicians quoting the results of research findings and basically justifying their case for grant aid. During the debate it became clear that there was a well-oiled poverty 'industry,' with Western suppliers lined up to clinch any grant aid available and politicians, with dubious motives, eager to co-operate if the price was right. My own position was that it was essentially a moral issue since there was (at that time at least) more than enough resources to go round. America in particular seemed reluctant to accept any suggestion of moral responsibility and stressed instead its role as a global leader in grant funding. It was strange to witness such insular thinking from such a usually far-sighted nation. And it was a lesson in how even the most enlightened of nations can have un-joined-up policies.

In New York I also took part in a yoga exhibition in a disused shop within a shopping mall. I also remember sitting in meditation with a woman in her mid-twenties who was wearing a semi-transparent, plastic jump suit. It appeared to me as though her body had become a mere commodity. Her face was drained and she looked exhausted, as though she had been sucked dry by New York nightlife. I was reminded how desperately some people are searching for peace and happiness. There but for the grace of God... Sadly, she was too far gone to benefit from meditation. The experience also reminded me of just how draining big city life can be as the struggle for the next high continues relentlessly. And then it was back to the UK via JFK Airport. I don't remember much about the flight back except the crying baby in the row in front. It cried virtually all the way back and proved a useful test of my power of tolerance.

Once back in the UK I found that I was experiencing a couple of emotions. On the one hand, I was happy to be back with my friends and on the other I had become quite used to the pioneering lifestyle which ended abruptly when I returned to the role of student. It seemed to me that I was returning to a situation that was not offering many opportunities for males to progress, unlike our female counterparts who were being sent to all corners of the world. It was a situation that contrasted with the colourful scenes I had grown used to. When I consider it now, I can see how ego might have played its part, but at the time it felt like I was an unfulfilled resource. In the absence of any other opportunities I threw myself into editing a book using my meditation very intensively for inspiration. On completion of the book the text was flatly rejected by Ninabhen who had been put in charge of publications. At the time it felt to me like a rejection of the validity of my yoga and served as yet one more reason to feel victimised, and even bitter, in a self-righteous kind of way. The book was published a couple of years later but by then I was set on another course.

Under the circumstances I thought it best to relocate to the Edinburgh Centre. However, when I arrived there, I found that the centre was now in the hands of a very young teacher who was clearly intimidated by my presence. As the most senior student in the Centre the other students naturally looked on me as an example. I knew that I couldn't be the example that I wanted to be. My health was still not good and I felt a need to withdraw from everything so that I could give the body time to rest and recover. In addition, I was not happy that opportunities for men seemed so few. It seemed to me that simply reversing the usual inequalities between the sexes was not taking us forward. I was aware that my unease about this issue was making me restless and this was not something I wished to pass on to the younger students.

A plan of action began to form in my head. With complete conviction it seemed to me that the solution that would be best for everyone was if I simply stepped out of the way. So, in the sincere conviction that I was doing the very best for those around me I made the decision to cut my connections with the Raja Yoga Centre and instead follow my own path. To make it clear that I had not lost my faith in what I had learned and that I hadn't become a victim of some evil temptation I travelled down one last time to the Centre in London and announced my plan to the senior teacher. She warned me that it was dangerous to get isolated in this way but I remained convinced that it was in everyone's best interest that I get out of the way of others. It was this conviction of service to others, however misguided it may have been, that was to make me so resolute in the years to come.

CHAPTER 5. GOING SOLO

Life away from my community was much more difficult than I had imagined. For a start the rest for body and soul that had seemed so appealing turned out to be a mere illusion. On reflection, I underestimated the extent that good yoga is founded upon good study. I thought that my previous learning would prove sufficient for my needs. I was mistaken. The mental stimulation that flows from regular changes of focus was missed more than I had anticipated.

But perhaps the most difficult aspect of my new situation was that I no longer seemed to fit in to 'normal life'. It was a bit like my earlier experience of being rejected, first by a privileged group and then by my workmates. My abnormality was expressed through my very pores. It had not occurred to me that in stepping away from an overtly yogic lifestyle I might not readily fit back into the normality I had so abruptly left behind five years before. In particular, forming any type of relationship, both with males and females was extremely difficult. I could pretend to be normal for a few sentences but thereafter my abnormality would spill out. It felt a bit like being a soldier returning from the trenches being unable to hold a normal conversation. My consciousness had changed as a result of all that I had seen and done and it was difficult to communicate my experiences to those who were just getting on with their lives.

There had not been the violence of the trenches but, I had seen things and gone through experiences that I knew were beyond the understanding of most of the people around me. In desperation, I decided to seek some counselling from the University of Edinburgh's Chaplain, who I knew to be a Roman Catholic priest. I suppose I was hoping that he might understand my celibacy pledge in a way that others wouldn't. It seemed to be a big deal for most people, who were prone to take a more Freudian position. When I related my story to him the priest's eyes lit up. I had forgotten that for most religious institutions a living experience of 'spirituality' is only an aspiration. Six months later, the priest himself was off to India in pursuit of his own experience. I never saw him again to inquire if he was successful.

My counselling didn't reveal much so I joined a men's development group which invited me to talk about a recent holiday as a way of introducing myself to the group. My recent holiday experience in North and South America apparently didn't fit the bill and it very quickly became obvious that this group was not a context in which I was going to experience much development. The focus of the group was on much more pragmatic issues. Another blank for me!

I was successful in getting a job, albeit as a local authority administration assistant. With a regular income I was able to give my life some badly needed structure, although I was still not happy with the direction in which things were moving. I was still meditating in the early hours of the morning though the quality of the experience was beginning to diminish. I felt that going to one of the Yoga Centres would be a backward step and not an option I wanted to take having made a clean break. So, the only way open to me, in my opinion at the time, was to move forward into the general community.

Even in my job it was proving difficult for me to fit in. My vegetarianism, in the early '80s, was a source of great controversy. "What's wrong with meat"? "What are you going to eat if you don't have sandwiches like the rest of us"? It was seen as a form of exhibitionism, a ploy to attract attention. My prediction that the climate would change, perhaps not a wise topic to share, was met with widespread derision in my workplace. At the time Edinburgh was not the cosmopolitan place it is now so maybe the learning was to just keep quiet. By the time I left that job eight years later I had fully grasped that normality demanded complete silence on issues relating to my past. Celibacy however continued to prove a contentious issue. It seemed as though it was causing a great deal of consternation (not to mention speculation) that I was not yoked in a twosome. I remember one of my co-worker's angry reaction to something I had said. "At least I've got a partner!". It seemed twosomes were a status symbol.

As far as I can remember of life in the early '80s, I continued with my habit of daily meditation. Needless to say, it was not very deep consisting largely of constant replay of the circumstances that had led me to my break from the pack. I still felt no desire to return. The blame for my circumstances lay elsewhere, or so I told myself. So, I remained convinced that I had done the right thing and, by now, I felt that any bridges had been well and truly burned.

In the mid '80s I began to think of what I could do with the rest of my life. I started leading two highly successful fitness classes at Edinburgh's Royal Commonwealth Pool. And I took a part-time job as a Community Education Tutor with another Local Authority. These jobs provided me with a distraction but not the depth of satisfaction I had known as a committed yogi.

Life as a sports coach 1982.

My full-time job was requiring me to act well below my capabilities but it provided me with the funds to make my first purchase of a flat in the city centre of Edinburgh. I also acquired a dog. If I was to survive without a human partner then canine company seemed like a good idea. So, I went to the local dog compound and took one of their strays. The regular dog-walks, three times a day, got me out of the flat though sometimes it was a burden.

I progressed in my job to become COSLA's training officer. COSLA was similar to a parliament for Scottish local authorities, providing a range of centralised services, including training. I was tasked with conducting training needs analysis for several of the more rural local authorities in Scotland. These training audits were designed to identify the specific training needs within each organisation. On the one hand it was a marvelous opportunity to intervene at a senior level in different authorities with very different cultures and structures, and on the other hand it made keeping a pet totally impossible as I was required to overnight in various rural towns around the country. I had a very difficult decision to make, my career or my pet? In the end my mortgage decided it. I couldn't afford to lose my job so the dog had to be rehoused! It was like losing a best friend.

The training audits involved working closely with chief executives which eventually led to me establishing a development group for chief executives which met a couple of times a year in different hotels across Scotland. These men, and they were all men at that time, were all trying to weigh up their resources in order to deliver services as best they could while at the same time following the political steer laid down by local Councilors who could, from time to time, prove difficult to manage.

Interestingly, they revealed doubts and fears in that peer group setting which were totally absent in more public situations. On the one hand, I knew that it was important to show due deference to the chief executives, and on the other I knew that I had witnessed realities that were well beyond the scope of these men. In this context the task was to stay small and play my part well!

After eight years of working in Edinburgh I knew it was time to move on. An interesting job as a Training Manager came up in the Highlands, based in Dingwall. I knew that the Chief Executive was one of the best in Scotland, even if the Authority was a bit sleepy. It was a job reporting directly to this Chief Executive and was specifically tasked with "cultural change." Cultural change was a topic that fascinated me and in a setting like the Highlands that had been so resistant to change throughout history the challenge would be even greater than ever.

After a successful interview, I set off from Edinburgh for a new start in the Highlands. Probably, like most visitors to the Highlands my first impression was of the awesome beauty of the place. I quickly learned that there were locals and there were 'incomers' who were tolerated if they didn't try to rock the boat. Unfortunately, I was there to rock the boat and so from the start I was met with traditional Highland resistance, silent and often uncooperative.

Having been quite popular throughout my life, it was a whole new experience being the subject of so much distrust. Over time, I began to win some people round but apart from the Chief Executive, who was nearly always supportive I didn't have many friends, and even had a few enemies. The words of Kipling's poem 'If' came to mind in that setting, particularly, "If you can bear to hear the truth you've spoken twisted by knaves to make a trap for fools." Departmental politics was always lively!

One very interesting development from this phase of my life was that I began to train in Neurolinguistic Programming. At first my intention was to increase my power as a communicator but over the course for my training, I began to understand that influence is gained through listening to people not talking at them. The multiple solutions to our multiple problems would emerge from our people on the front line not from anyone at the top. Elected members and their senior managers would decide in which areas we needed solutions. This was policy-driven from the top. But the people on the front line were usually best placed to decide in what form those solutions should be.

Neurolinguistic Programming (NLP) will probably be new to most readers, so I'll say a few words about it as it will be referred to several times. NLP is the study of the thinking and language patterns that shape our behavioural patterns (programmes). If someone chooses to change their behaviour, NLP offers the skills to support that with appropriate thoughts and language. Often people were initially hostile towards NLP which they tended to see as potentially intrusive but they usually became enthusiastic when they saw its' benefits.

Meanwhile, in my new Highland bungalow, perched high on the hill above the village of Beauly, it rapidly became apparent to me that I really had not much interest in transforming the new house into a home. Form-filling and checking bank details held no fascination for me. "Nest-building" was quite frankly beyond my level of competency. Very fortunately, at about this time, I met the woman who was to become my wife. Where I was still a bit detached from the machinations of the "real" world, she was intimately au fait with them. Where I was introverted and socially ill at ease, she was extrovert and socially adept.

But, above all, she struck me as a soul who needed stability and love, two things I felt able to offer her. Together, we were able to live very comfortably and very successfully, albeit with quite different world views. We set up home together in the Victorian spa village of Strathpeffer, eight miles west of Dingwall and fifteen north of Inverness.

Wedding in Poolewe, in the Scottish Highlands, 1992.

Our much-loved home in beautiful Strathpeffer

In 1996, I took voluntary redundancy from local government having become disillusioned with the internal politics of large organisations. I decided to start my own training and business consultancy primarily based on NLP.

Publicity shot for my new business.

It wasn't long before I was invited to serve on another management team, a training company in Buckinghamshire with whom I had previously trained. However, before long this arrangement in the South of England began to cause stress in my life, involving very early flights to Heathrow, hired cars and late-night homecomings. I was also mixing with people from a part of the country with very different values about money and business protocol. It was not a scenario I enjoyed and I was, frankly, very pleased to resign and escape from that whole situation. I had, nevertheless, gained some very useful experience and got my foot in the door of some very interesting companies.

Some enlightened GPs recognised the extent to which certain diseases, both mental and physical, are the product of poor neurological programming. In other words, unhelpful patterns of thought, dysfunctional behavioural patterns or behaviour that was not properly aligned with thinking. As an option to prescribing drugs some GPs would sometimes refer these clients to me. As a consequence, I began to build up experience of working with clients from a wide range of medical backgrounds, each presenting symptoms that were in some way functional for them even if not for the rest of the world.

I formed a 'learning community' that also met a couple of times a year in different hotels around Scotland. Our aim was to provide long-term learning support to our former NLP students. About a dozen of us would meet up for this purpose.

Other activities around this time involved providing management training for the Scottish Executive, now The

Lunchtime with a group of trainees at Edinburgh University

Scottish Government, over a four-year period. As well as providing some of my most satisfying work this group also provided my most challenging work being an organisational culture where stoicism (dissociated behaviour) is often the norm.

The cancellation of the Inverness-Heathrow route put an end to our time in the Highlands because a lot of my work was in the South of England. We left our beloved house in the village of Strathpeffer; With a twinge of sadness we headed south towards the more crowded beauty of the city of Edinburgh. After several unsuccessful housing bids in the city we eventually found a small house in the market town of Haddington, about 25 miles to the east of Edinburgh. We thought at the time it would serve as a base from which to launch our Edinburgh operation. In fact, it's still the family home today though I am now unable to access much of it with my wheelchair and live instead in supported accommodation in the city of Edinburgh.

In 2002 I travelled to the US, initially to attend a business conference in Santa Fe. There was sufficient interest in a project that I was working on regarding eldership and wisdom that I got distracted from my business in the UK. I had noticed the vital role elders play in traditional societies, steering the youth and taking a long-term view on current issues. I held the view that it might be possible to coach elderly Americans to exert this kind of influence on US institutions. At that time, I was inspired by the writings of Neale Donald Walsh; in particular his ideas about self-expression. I traveled throughout the southwest of the US. for the best part of two years with scarcely a thought about my responsibilities back home. With hindsight this was an influence that distracted me from achieving my goals in life. In fact, I'd go further than that and say it was a chapter in my life that was positively harmful in that my focus moved away from serving others. It was only when I had my stroke in 2005, and was unable to play with words, that it was completely apparent to me that the Neale Walsh's "Conversations with God" books had nothing to offer me beyond clever wordplay.

The Wisdom and Eldership project (which formed the basis for my second book, 'Some Really Useful Hints for a Successful Life') never really took off in the US because everyone involved was looking at it from the perspective of how the project could generate money or fame for them and there was little belief that the elderly could contribute anything of meaning to any project involving wisdom. Even the American equivalent of Age UK intimated that "old folks are only interested in the size of their pensions, their welfare benefits and holiday cruises".

And so, I returned to the UK disappointed at my failure to spark imaginations but enriched by some of the people I had met along the way. It was now 2003 and I struggled to pick up where I had left off. I was running my business right through to 2005 when my life was turned upside down by my stroke which doctors told me was caused by a genetic predisposition to create harmful cholesterol. My initial reaction was panic because so many life-long skills were suddenly not working. There was nevertheless the assumption that 'this too will pass' and that medicine would restore the situation. But when in time a critical point was reached, the awareness dawned that this could be the curtain call.

So, let's get back to life in hospital. As I've already mentioned, I was unable to continue my lifelong habit of daily meditation. As a consequence, I was able to see myself acting without its' modifying influence. And it wasn't a pretty sight. Old patterns of negative thinking had begun to re-emerge and in a hospital setting, where waiting for things is the default situation, I had become openly cynical about what the NHS had to offer.

When I finally got back to my new supported accommodation, I found myself wondering what purpose my continued breathing might serve. It was clear that I would be unable to return to my former career. Or any other career for that matter. Previously my work had provided me with a sense of purpose, but what now? I was trapped in an uncooperative body, placing a burden on family and, more generally, on society itself. I had ceased to be a contributor to society. I was no longer in a position to influence the direction of its travel which was something that had been very important to me in the past. Whether or not I had any success in that regard is a moot point.

I had the recurring feeling that I ought to be at some event somewhere around the globe. When I realised that was not true there would follow a deep frustration. As one visitor to my flat put it my world, which had once been so big, had become very small. This was full-blown existential anxiety!

I would suddenly awaken to my circumstances and find myself sitting on the margins of society in a body that bore no relation to the one I had grown used to over the years. When there was a physical symptom I would catastrophize, imagining that the symptom was the precursor to something much worse. I had lost confidence in the body's capacity to maintain its equilibrium, so every symptom had the potential to erupt into something much more serious. By this stage I had experienced a brain-stem stroke, a heart attack, MRSA, gangrene, pneumonia, two collapsed lungs, acute renal failure, a deep vein thrombosis and resuscitation after a blood loss. Was my hypochondria really medical vigilance? Who knows?

My inability to influence events in a world, which in my opinion was in desperate need of influencing, led me to the decision to communicate with everything at my disposal. This was never going to be easy with no functional speech and with severely restricted body language. First, came my art which was encouraged and supported by some excellent staff in my day centre. At their request this initiative culminated in a city centre

An advert for the Glasgow performance.

art exhibition and the sale of several paintings. Then came two books, the first of which was adapted into a play format and shown in Edinburgh and Glasgow.

With Adam Tomkins, the actor who played me on-stage.

And finally, I was asked to write a blog post. After a dozen or so articles I got tired of hearing my own 'voice' and brought the blog to an end. But who knows, maybe someone was influenced along the way!

In 2009 I renewed my contact with the Edinburgh Raja Yoga Centre, although daily attendance at class was no longer an option for logistical reasons. It was at one of their celebrations, when people were giving glowing accounts of how their lives had been turned around by the various disciplines of Raja Yoga, that I first became aware of the bitterness I had un-knowingly been carrying around for several decades. For the very first time I saw how I had allowed petty things to dominate the course of my life! I also had the opportunity to speak to some of the ex-students of the Edinburgh Centre and it seemed that London's failure to recognise Scotland as a separate country had been one of the factors that had frustrated them, as I had suspected 30 years earlier.

I also began to think about faith. I had managed to avoid the development of complete faith by keeping alive a small element of doubt in the entire project. I had convinced myself that there was total faith but now I was coming to the understanding that faith is multi-layered like the proverbial onion. I had given most of my life following, as best I could, the teachings of Raja Yoga. I readily accept that I was far from a good example of a regular student. I realised that I had unconsciously taken the viewpoint of a sociologist, always placing my own beliefs alongside competing belief systems. This was very laudable for those studying comparative religion but for someone aiming to progress as a Raja Yogi it was a major deficiency.

But most importantly of all I saw the big picture again. We're living in a broken world. Day by day the various institutions that have managed crises in the past have shown themselves to be inadequate to manage the scale of the challenges that lie ahead. People are, quite reasonably, anxious. The entire world is peaceless at a time when the world needs all the peace and love it can get. And maybe what the world needs most is happiness. It's not time to fixate on petty issues. I recognise that this is an important time. There's a lot that needs to change in the world and as Ghandi pointed out, that change has to start with me. I would like to tell you how the story ends but the final chapter has not yet been written, (although Covid-19 is working darned hard to change that!). So, like me, you'll just have to wait and see. One thing is for sure though, it has most definitely been a life less ordinary so far.

The image of light I now use in meditation to still the mind.

Further Information

Previous Publications:

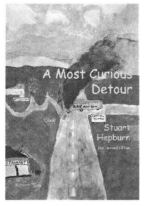

"A Most Curious Detour,"

ISBN 978-1-4457-8896-8

Available for £6.99 from Amazon

"Some Really Useful Hints for a Successful Life."

ISBN 978-1-4477-1086-8

Available for £4.99 From Lulu Publishing

100% of the proceeds from all three books goes to registered charities.

To contact the author: lessord9@gmail.com

For more information about Raja Yoga **0131 229 7220**

ABOUT THE AUTHOR

Stuart Hepburn was born and educated in Edinburgh. However, his family home is in the beautiful market town of Haddington.

For a number of years, a Yogic monk in India, he regressed by stages to running his own business focused on management and training consultancy.

Following a brain-stem stroke in 2005 at the age of 52, which left him severely disabled and without a functioning voice he has lived in supported accommodation back in Edinburgh. He is now permanently ensconced in his throne, an electric wheelchair.

He is the author of A Most Curious Detour, (2010) and Some really Useful Hints for a Successful Life, (2011).

Printed in Poland
by Amazon Fulfillment
Poland Sp. z o.o., Wrocław